T0153251

WHALE AND VAPOR

고래와 수증기

Whale and Vapor

by Kim Kyung Ju
Translated by Jake Levine

Black Ocean
Boston · Detroit · Chicago

Black Ocean
P.O. Box 52030
Boston, MA 02205
blackocean.org

Cover Art and Design by Abby Haddican | abbyhaddican.com
Book Design by Nikkita Cohoon |ritualmorningstudio.com

ISBN 978-1-939568-30-4

This book was published with the support of the Literature Translation Institute of Korea.

Cataloging in Publication data available at the Library of Congress.

Library of Congress Control Number:
2020931994

FIRST EDITION

CONTENTS

I

POET BLOOD

I I
FEET LEFT AFTER BEING BURNED

I I I
I KNOW

I V

FEET ALWAYS COLD LIKE YOU

TRANSLATOR'S PREFACE

1.　　Notes on the book

Kim Kyung Ju's first book of poetry *I Am a Season that Does Not Exist in the World* begins with a painter who is born without limbs. Painting with his mouth, he spends his entire life painting a world in which he goes searching for a color no one has discovered. It is within that imaginary world where he finds his missing limbs. In this way, he creates a frame for the power of art to redeem and make whole what is otherwise imperfect or deformed. Even though it is anti-lyric, it is an incredibly romantic book. In Korea *I Am a Season that Does Not Exist in the World* is considered to be one of the most important books of poetry of the early 2000's. Kyung Ju, along with the poets Kim Minjeong and Hwang Byung-sng, were considered to be the pioneers of a new style of poetry called Miraepa (future-wave) in Korean. That movement was created in the momentum of economic restructuring that resulted from the IMF crisis. It signaled a break in tradition and history, both in literature and in culture at large. It was a scary time. But it was also an exciting time.

Kim Kyung Ju's most recent poetry collection, *Whale and Vapor* (published in Korean in 2014) also has a poem featuring a painter. The painter in this poem creates a world that others don't understand. The town he paints on the canvas becomes a place where his brushes go to die, where the painter loses himself. The poems in *Whale and Vapor* incorporate a sense of repetition that is influenced by the father of contemporary Korean poetry, Kim Soo Young. Like Kim Soo Young, the repetition in Kyung Ju's poems mirrors the theme of exhaustion. This perhaps has much to do with the historical and political circumstances in Korea when the book was being written. Park Geun Hye, the daughter of the former military dictator Park Chung Hee was elected president in 2012. It was a dark time. These poems are playful, but a lot of the romanticism and hope of the earlier work has been dimmed by that experience. However, the turn toward the lyric might be a way in which Kyung Ju reconciles losing the idealism of his early work. It is a turn toward tradition, toward Kim Soo Young, and his literary ancestry.

2.   Notes on the translation

I think there are some parallels between the experience of watching a subtitled movie and reading a translated book. When you translate the dialogue and put it into a text that people are reading at the bottom of the screen, the words get pulled out from the actor's mouth. The audience's experience is mediated by an outside interpreter, a voice that exists in excess of the movie. However, even if they can't understand it, the audience can hear the original language. I think reading a translation of a poem is somewhat similar to watching a subtitled movie. I'm mediating your experience of these poems, not in substitute of the original, but in addition to the original. In that vein, I don't think there is such a thing as accurate translation. There is no equivalent; the translation exists separately and as a compliment. Translation is weird in that way. It is creative but not independent. It begins with collaboration.

Kyung Ju and I have gone on reading tours together in the United States, England, and Scotland. When we read we try to create a dramatic dialogue between the translation and the original. The way in which we come up with our performance has to do with the way in which he reads the poems. Part of my process in translating is to have Kim read his poems aloud. The way in which he adds stress, pauses, and performs his work has been very important to the way in which I have translated the energy and feeling of the poems. As much as translation has to do with capturing the nuance and meaning of the content on the page, it is just as important to mimic the performance of the text in air, to try and score the music of the language similarly. Syntactically, I tried to mimic the original as much as possible.

Because translation begins with collaboration, I want to take some time here to thank some people without whom this book wouldn't have been possible. I want to thank Hedgie Choi and Soeun Seo who looked over this manuscript and corrected many of my mistakes. I also received much moral support from my friends and colleagues Jen Hui Bon Hoa and Richard Greenfield. I wish to thank the writer Hailji for introducing me to Kyung Ju when I first arrived in Korea in 2012. Thanks to Toad Press and Clinic Presents for putting out chapbooks from this book, and thanks to *Granta*, *Bat City Review*, and *Poetry London* for publishing individual poems. I also want to thank Janaka Stucky and Carrie Olivia Adams for their friendship, vision, and support. Thank you to my colleagues at both the Korean Literature Translation Institute and Keimyung University, and Claire Kyung Jin in particular. Thanks to Jorge García Pellicer, who put me up in Barcelona for two months while

I was editing this manuscript. And finally, thanks to Kim Kyung Ju, my brother and collaborator for many years now. You are the ventriloquist and I, the dummy. When I am mouthing the words, I often hear your voice when I am talking.

ī

-

POET BLOOD

What a nice room to get altitude sickness in.
I go to the forest
to get bit by a red, venomous snake.

SWEEP UP A FLOCK

Like the sound of washing calves in cold water
a bird flock takes flight.

A mountain ridge hangs on the calves of a flock of birds.
Wild roses bloom on the calves of a flock of birds.

Clouds will drip the smell of skin

until birds pass through my body.
Even this, I believe, is the work of passing birds.

Clouds float down.
They sip water in the valley.

I sweep up a flock of birds.

LET ME IN

Among my thousands of names
my saddest name
is you.

When I first saw you
sleeping on white snow
I quietly crawled beside you.

When I first saw you
I put on my pajamas and
followed you
into your pajamas
and huddled.

Even when I'm scared I don't make a sound
when I love you and
because I'm scared I don't make a sound
when I love you.

I have thousands of names.
My saddest name
is the name you call me.

SNOWBLIND

When the newspaper stopped delivery
I got wrapped with birds.

When the water got shut off
I became water
rolling down the hills.

When people lost touch
I became a pigeon perched
on a sunflower.

When aphasia set in
I turned into atmosphere.

In the morning you look for a word
inside my body.
In the morning
I look for vapor within your body.

A stone that gives up eating
becomes transparent in the sun.

When wind dies
heaven climbs a mountain.

MORON

When a stray dog is a moron
it dances.

Atop the sea
an empty phone booth
floats.

A climber stranded on the cliff
takes a map out of his chest.
He blows at the gorge
and pushes the map away.

Flying canyons

swell with boulders.
Quietly
a pencil is sharpened.
The eraser gets shaved.

Sunlight dozes off standing up
and falls asleep beneath your feet.

Painted with ink, the white
heavy rain.

FLESH PASSING IN THE SUN

I have
the leather of a seal
that you love.
Someday
I will go and see
seals again.
Sitting on a glacier
like a seal hunched over its front paws
I let out
a long-drawn yawn.
On a day that is lonely
like your black flesh
I memorize deep sea fish
instead of mountain peaks.
When the moon holds water in its mouth
it glows whiter
and floats away slower.
I bleed on a flock of birds.
While I wait for you
I'll climb this tiny iceberg
and take the seagull that flew here
and ferment it in my mouth.
I'll wait for you
until my flesh passes in the sun.

WITHOUT A TRACE

When a sentence gets caught on a flock of birds

it often makes a sound.

A sentence has to climb down from my face but
like cheeks that don't match their face

the sentence misses the sound parade
and heads into torchlight.
It stays up all night
without making a sound.

You've got to make peace with my chaos.
It's a chaos no one understands.

Birds in my dream
drool on my pillow
like my tilted face
drips spit.

My home away from home is
a sentence written in bird spit.

That sentence
left me here
without a trace.

MUG CUP

That bird that sat on that wall
left its legs when it flew away.

Like a rat that vanished
leaving two feet
caught in a trap,

two feet remain.

A mannequin sits
in a warm bath
melting.

Like the melting pupils of a mouse
that ate poison

every night
my mannequin
is unaware its feet melt
while it lathers its body with soap.

You live like me
with nothing
but static electricity and eyelashes.

On the wall, in the bath, in the trap

two remaining feet and
the static electricity
I want to keep covered up.

REINDEER ON MY UPPER LIP

Reindeer walk my upper lip
licking ice under their feet as they walk.

I lick the watery soles of someone's feet
that bulge beneath the ice.

Reindeer graze my upper lip, nibbling
the cold roots of a tree and the green leaves
that bud out the horns
of a reindeer calf that froze to death.

One time a baleen whale
breached my upper lip.
When my ears went hot the ice began to melt
and the reindeer carefully licked the flapping whale.
Under the leaves that stack my upper lip
the reindeer do not make love.

They sit on my upper lip and
wait until the horizon freezes to their tongues.
Sorrowfully, they mumble to themselves.

I was born on the fins of eyes.
Dragged into a snowy country, I became

the soft petroglyphs left by a pessimist.
One at a time
I dropped my eyelashes on the ice
to mark a path back home.

Reindeer lose themselves in line.
They fall asleep standing on ice.
In spring they become warm ice on the top of my lips.
They become my lips that melt below thin ice.

At the edge of the cliff on my lips
reindeer live dangerous.

AURORA

for the poet Kim Jeong Hwan

Sound floats inside a bird.
Like a bird floating in sound
before the bird touches down
a fir tree floats around momentarily.

A cloud floats on the forehead of a sleeping deer.
Like a white rice cake
floating on the dinner table
I float on the palm of my hand.

Water floats inside dead fish
like flocks of birds floating
in the mouth of a sinking whale.

Saltwater will float on my ten fingernails
before I die and
my feet will float for a bit
before you die.

If you gather your breath
a white moon floats inside your mouth.

If you hold your breath inside your lips
your belly floats like a boat.

POET BLOOD

The poet's role is to play breath.
He flows through every spot on the stage
and disappears into another role.
The poet's destiny
is like the secret of a cat missing its paw.
He appears and disappears
never revealing himself to the audience.
Breath is born infinitely and yet
it must remain hidden.
Each day the poet evaporates inside the breath he creates,
making playgrounds with breath.
His entire life is wasted
trying to arrange a parade made of breathing.
Like a cat that laughs while hiding its paw,
a siren rings around in search of breath
wanting to be born secretly.

Wandering inside all the breath on stage,
a breath realizes it doesn't have long to live.
It disappears into a place no one can know.
Some people believe that if they erase the date of their birth and death
they will find equality.
Breath enters the sentence it builds.
It quietly floats away.

THUNDER

Inside a cloud, alone
thunder roams
until it goes white with shock.

Thunder touches the tongue of a stray dog.

The single face of someone
I can't remember—
If someone builds a fire
I want to go inside it
and find a face.
Even fire is colder than me.

The empty bags I carry around are cold.
Your office building
has many kinds of doors, but
I know the sewers that
lead to your shiny garden.

The few seconds of a kiss and
the flame of a few candles and
the few minutes of flight
are my war's front line.

Into a nature you don't know
I go white with fear.

Stray dogs licking
the underbelly of the frozen corpse of a deer, the thunder

that touches the tongues of stray dogs.

On the underbelly of a dead deer
sleeping birds get scared.

Like a rumor born
by pushing someone off a cliff

my body itches.
A traveler is about to jump.

THE 13 PHASES OF THE MOON

January Moon
Forest

I'm buried in the forest.
My voice turns into water.
Roots drink up the night.

February Moon
Shadow

Game of shadows.
The scent of bougainvillea
follows a white wall, walking.
A match strikes the white wall and
inside the shadow's chest
one rib gets plucked.

March Moon
Sunshine

City campsite.
Green bugs gathered by hand
roast on the grill.
A kid selling forsythia.

More than baking flour,
I am so soft.

April Moon
Sleet

The cap of a forest ranger
lost in a canyon
on fire.
A frog left in a desk drawer in the classroom all winter.
Inside a mirror
the frog's head puckers out.

May Moon
Secret Pocket

A pocket turned inside out.
I liked the smell.
One night I clipped out the pocket
and buried it in the ground.
I'm your comfortable interior.

June Moon
Helmet

I want to laugh like you.
Painting my eyebrows economically,

I want to break a bone.
I whisper secrets to the broken bone.
A hospital gets demolished.
In its place, a helmet shop.

July Moon
Night

The sun at night is sweet
until the spoon melts.

Mid-July Moon
Bakery

The neighborhood bakery
has faith in wheat.
Bread fresh out the oven
like a cream white lie.
When the final bread arrives, I'll be there to break it with you.
Cats rip apart rancid cartons of milk.
I wake up in the middle of you.

August Moon
Crocodile

A friend is headed to the mountain.
He drags along a disabled child.

He's going to lick the child's ears.
I couldn't stop him even if I tried.
Touching a numb chin
with a face like it made a promise,
a night of shoving your head in a toilet and
puking up a green crocodile.

August Moon
Hydraulic Shovel

A tree that drowned
in the water
dragged out by a hydraulic shovel.
A wild cherry tree sitting on the sofa
dreaming a somnolent dream.

September Moon
Zoo

For 15 minutes I lie next to the giraffe
because the giraffe lies down for 15 minutes.
The zoo on a rainy day.
To look at the balloon
that let go of my hand
the giraffe sinks quietly.

October Moon
Coins

The dim sound of coins.
Galloping outside the window
coming to take the bride.
Even though you can't touch a soft insect
you can probably kill
a hard one.
That is, if the coin is dim.

November Moon
Moon

Above my eyes, a creeping snake.
I'm here, where I've disappeared, what remains.
The final arrangement.
I paint a wave headed toward the moon in my notebook.
I go to sleep.

December Moon
Bird

Footprints of birds stamp
in the shadow of an elongating sun.
The low mountains bloom in my pocket.
On the rock face of North America

I dingle dangle. I hang.

The Thirteenth Moon

The forest where I was buried.
My voice that became water.
You chirping.

A REALLY OLD FAREWELL

I like a forest that has evidence of a fire.
The smell of ants blackened in the sun.

I like grass with a lot of husks. Fossils have kind hearts.
They only appear in empty time. In empty time
a short flame can thin.

I like the ficus planted inside the sneakers you left behind.
If I open my eyes, I go inside a big jar and roll around.
I come to a halt in front of a hill.

Filled with silence, I like the empty endings of my words.
Like the necks of giraffes that live inside wallpaper,

a dim smudge is left by a finger on a pull-up bar. The silence
of a hand loosening its grip is good. Because I am a dark stadium,
carefully, you press a thumb inside my mouth.

AFFECTIONATE DEPRESSIONS

Not at your house, the pots
are at my house.
The bowls you collect,
the silverware I carry.
You gather soft pillows
and I gather narrow sleeves.
For you there is a beefy motorcycle and
for me there is a gentle edge.
The smell you don't have
is the smell I have.
When the ladle burns black
I start to cry but
you make a delicious meal anyway.
We can't wake our mom
who sleeps in the armoire.
Even if we throw the armoire in some alleyway
our mom will still be inside.
Inside that house
we dried out like fruit knives.
Not at your house,
the hatreds are in my house.
Sundays for me were too many
and I had too many dads.
I wanted to hurt

the women whose hair you touched.
Not for you,
the names of buttons are for me.
Like me, call the cats that crouch
Black Warm Earmuff.
The keys I hold tight in my sleep
are like blue tropical fish.
When the light switch gets flipped
my sisters cover their ears
inside the blanket stuffing.

I JUST CRY

With its side burst
the whale with a blue scar
that came floating toward the beach
makes me cry.

Taking a ladle of hot soup over
to the lips of the injured whale,
the boy that pours soup, and the spit
dribbling out the corner of the whale's mouth
makes me cry.

"I'll take you home."
Because of the retartedness
of these two people kissing in the snow
I cry and I don't know why.

*

Because of the season of the high school girl
who lived several months
inside a water tank
on an apartment rooftop
after she ran away from home,
I cry.

"I'm scared..."
"Today I'm going home too..."
Because the death report said
that girl was found floating around like a canary
with millions of plastic wrappers for bread
inside the yellow water tank
that filled up with water,
I cry.

*

For the naivety of the kid
who ripped off his house's nameplate and kicked it just for fun,
who never knew his dad who ran away after winning the lottery,
I cry.

Making heaven inside their mouths and
hiding the northern gates of the moon,
for those government officials
that grow fat inside their ears,
I cry.

*

Leaving everything behind
while not stopping for anything,
because of the intellectual hideout

of the rhetoric of those who like burning sugar
on the genitals of poets,
I cry.

*

Over-rushed, we fall in love at first sight.
Those words make me cry.
Because of the weariness of the philosopher
who says he will never look at poetry again,
taking out his anger on a piece of paper,
I cry.

*

At some point newspapers became something
used for drying flowers.
If you collect old papers and put them in the sun, I thought
the humidity will fly off, the noise will go away, the letters
will shed their scent and
their soft valleys
will be like indoor chrysanthemums or mountain chrysanthemums
    or asters;
they will endure this violent age, so I kept them.
But this morning the headline is

Poetry Collections Are Cheap

It makes me cry.
I, just.

CONTEMPORARY LITERATURE

I try to think about my love's reaction and
the side effect you have of disappearing.

If you take aim at life
the skin of the arrow tapers.
If you aim at death
the blood of the target dims.

Your pockets fill up
with eraser dust.

ALTOCUMULUS CLOUDS

Clouds crowd together
into drops of water.

The insides of clouds bunch up.
Night blows.

In my monthly publication
the clouds that crowd together
burst with birds.

A sentence resembles the life of a cloud.
A word makes the clouds pulse.
The morning counts
the lives of words,
the tranquil dust of rocks that belong to the sun,
and tears that resemble my life.
These things the morning calls human.

Those drops
go and hide
like deer.

Night turns
drops of water into

the loneliest
buoyancy on earth.
The clouds transport
a sadness not yet born.

Crowding together, water drops.

ii

-

FEET
LEFT
AFTER
BEiNG
BURNED

SNOW FALLING IN WATER

—Poet Blood 2

White teeth shine
like sorrowful nuptials.

In winter my teeth
are white like a snake that stayed up all night.

Blue snow inside my mouth
falls in summer.

Down to the bottom of the sea
my snowflakes
dive deep.
They hold their breath.

FEET LEFT AFTER BEING BURNED

—Byeokje

I open the crematorium kiln.
Two feet remain.

People quietly cover their face.
I put the feet back in the kiln and start the flame.

Flowing out from the kiln,
body porridge boils over.
People plug their noses
at that rancid smell.
The rice I planted in the mouth is ripening.
With mouths full of white rice, people
think about the pupils
of the man in the kiln.

I open the kiln.
The beach the corpse washed up on
gets dredged with a shovel.
People turn their heads. They shut their eyes.

I open the kiln.
During this light and sturdy holiday
two feet wash up. They sit on the coast.
Snow falls inside the kiln.

THE TREE THAT BECAME
A PIANO 4

—for Jake Levine

Today
a tree opened up
on the moon for the very first time.

Today
is for making pianos
out of a tree
that was brought down to earth.

Today
a drop of water
that fell from the moon
became a sea
inside the piano.

Today
snails live in a tiny hole
trying to lick moisture from their bodies.

I trust that you will embrace me.

THE NARRATIVE ARC OF A FIGURE OF A HAND

A hand heads toward the wall.
Birds gush out the hand.
The hand gains altitude
in the dark.
If we open our eyes in our hands
we become a pair in the dawn.
The bird born in a hand
can't know itself.
I'm a feather with many secrets.
Like the bird inside the wall
that doesn't know where it is,
I wildly flap inside a bird.
Today I call the bird that sits
at the end of my finger *you*.
Poetry sits at the elevation of the tips
of my fingers.
Like birds that look for a flock
they can't recognize themselves flying in,
a pair of hands can't feel
their altitude in the dark.
One hand becomes a bird
that wants to cover your face.
The other hand is your hand.

I want to hide your hand
because it touched me.
What kind of human are you?
Eyes closed, I
in a sinking field.

THE REASON I TURN MY BACK AND WALK AWAY

—for Harim

I turn my back and walk away

because the glimmering molars thrown on my roof
are up there still.
When spring arrives, without fail
migratory birds will lick the haze above my forehead.

I turn my back and walk away.

My mumblings fly out my body like wild ducks every night.
They are trivial for you.
I look at wind flowing beneath the stomachs of a flock of birds at night.
This unlimited affection fattens my pupils

I turn my back and walk away.

There is a night sky that can only be seen
by entering your breath. I'm hanging on it.
Into that triviality, a limitless cliff,
the snow that falls turns blue.

Forlorn grass sways its hips.
Because of all this
I turn my back and walk away.

You sat on the floor all day
with one breast cut off
and bit an empty spoon.
Because a sentence rose
from the cold breath of a deer
that collapsed in a forest, its ankle twisted,

I turn my back to walk away.

Because sadness always carries neatly arranged secrets,
but this is too good a world for mingling,
I cannot become lonely by myself,
so I stop.
The most tenacious people live on the ground floor.

If there's any rest for us, it'll be with that kind of volition.

CROSS EYED

—Poet Blood 3

Because the pupil in your eye is cold
it can't live with other pupils.
Like an illegal alien
your pupil secretly escapes our field of sight.
Written in the tense we got deported to
your gaze peddles the world
on the black market.
However, at night
the cold returns to my eyes. It surges up.
Our vision your eyes see is pitiful.
We can't stare directly into your pupils.
It doesn't matter what field of vision our eyes are in
when we don't know where to look.
That space is too small for our eyes to meet.
It's not easy to shrink pupils with ridicule.
Even though your pupils aren't a target for love,
your world is in the place that is farthest from our gaze.
Inside our field of vision
your pupils move around the place that is most free.
In the field of vision where consent was received,
we are horrendous.

Like twins born without eyes
who spend their entire life not recognizing each other,
like twins that were born with one eye each
who spend their entire lives missing each other's bodies,
because we look in the same direction
our gazes never meet.
Two sets of eyes aren't the most distant from each other,
but they run to the place that is furthest away.
We smile with our eyes.
I guess that's what you call gazing.

POET BLOOD 4

No one
will hurt you
under this blanket.

Sentences
aren't introduced
to each other.
The images
that arrive
to register their birth

sparkle
like earth
seeped in the mantle.

Like deer horns
are ambiguous,
like a chimney without a pipe
is travelling

wherever things fall
hurt the eyes
like dice.
Can you pick me up

secretly?
I like spit
at the park.
I like
soap bubbles
that roll along
without feet.
A room that no one knows
is a room whose rent is paid.

That room gets clutched
by the talon of a hawk.
It gets brought here
like a bubble of soap.

SEASONAL INTERVALS

Even now when mom visits a stranger's house
she pokes her head inside their fridge.
I knew when she used to do it
because she would come home angry.
Mom's diary, I secretly peek in it every time I go back home.
Becoming curious, things get more personal.
Doing it lovelessly.

My lips leave your lips.
You secretly steal spoons every time we visit a cafe.
Like mother's spelling,
an elegant klepto is vibrant like a beggar's brimmed cap.

All the news in the world is travel writing.
Tomorrow no one will be able to remember the scoop.
I used to go around memorizing the names of victims
that are forgotten after their accidents.
I belong to your family lineage.
Dealing with a lineage that gets erased day by day, departing,
the spaces between my lines are full of life.
Every day I shit for a long time.
This is how my weather gets read.
My fake name appears in your forecast.
I'm into your vanity.

Have I ever loved anyone who wasn't vain?
Without manners,
I draw our lips eating pudding after we crawl under the blanket.

If you cut the toenails of a beast, the beast gets agitated.
Avoiding our signature like that beast,
we meet in the darkness.
Life is the process of enduring this delicate difference.
Doing it shamelessly.

I beat toward the heart of the mixed blood child I gave birth to.
In the end, even if I erase its name,
my child will come to the light.

Me and my forecast are already in the process of separating.
I will go on living my life complaining about my banality.
Even though I will miss it, irritably.

POETRY COMPOSITION

—a thousand steps

The breath of dried ants
laid down
after kids
brought them here
on the backs of their hands
is a different name
that belongs to the night.

The name of some dew
that carries my flesh
is the house that birds began to build
in a notebook.

When I put socks on my hands
and fall asleep
the tears that don't come
around visiting
are the names of orphans
I created.

Like the way
a flock of white birds
appear on the tongue
when you wake from a sleep
you slept while grinding your teeth

I can't return to speech
with exhaled breath.

That name
is a flock of dried birds
that passed into the sound of breathing
last night.

OBSCENITIES

I spread open my mouth in front of the mirror.
The afterlife lives inside my mouth.

The afterlife is in the mirror.

The man who spreads his mouth
and stands in front of the mirror
peeks at the afterlife vacantly.

Only one of his eyes
is headed to the afterlife in his mouth.
Because one eye is still on this side,
the language of the afterlife is in his mouth.

If I close my mouth
I close the afterlife too.

Right now the afterlife
is not some distant world,
but this world's language.

The mirror is the material property
made to show us the afterlife.
The language of this world

that walks into the mouth
inside the mirror
is our eyes.

Like silence
the afterlife can't avoid language.
It lives inside our mouths.

NATIONAL HIGHWAY

A fragment of a bird bone
whose wing joint
got pulled off.

Dried blood
on the floor.

A bird
with a fish in its mouth
puts the fish on its foot.

A bird
brings a stone in its mouth
and puts the stone on the fish's back.

If you rub my scales
with your feathers
they become leaking air.

A wave climbs
on top of the foot.

The fish
sinks into stone.

Birds are salty.

I HAVE HEART AS MUCH AS I DON'T HAVE A NAME...

Like a dry gold tooth
inside the mouth

a hawfinch
distantly
crouches
into the gold
of a field.

Filling up
with water,
a shed
opens its eyes
alone.

If you wear
a black dress
you can become
lonely too.

Blood is sweet and
birds bend too.

MY (UNDERWEAR)

atop a rice field
in Venice
a dead crane
flowing by

like underwear
someone secretly took off
slowly
flowing by

THE GREAT PANSORI SINGER

A worker shovels with the furnace open.
He chucks a snake into the furnace mouth.
Look at that snake crying in the light of the fire,
the fire at the fins of the racing steam train,
building the tension of funky smelling steam, building like pressure
    about to burst.
The worker who shoveled snakes into the mouth
releases the sticks of his hourglass drum. He jumps on the tracks.
He says he saw a fish rip its way out a snake.
Even though the snake became alcohol, the snake sings a song.
Your sound becomes rock dust from a different planet.
Future heat waves
will be called "The land
where the snake spat out its white Adam's apple."
Future snowstorms
will be called
"Snakeskin that crawled to the moon."
While watching
a black meteor crawl out its mouth,
a snake put his ears to the rail and cried.
That's the sound he makes
when a red-hot train rolls over his body.

STRENGTH OF TESTIMONY

The arsonist who shook the world got caught.

In front of the judge in the court where he was booked
he got asked "Why did you burn so many things?"

"I couldn't help it,"

the blind arsonist said.
Never once was he able to see his flame.

iii

-

i KNOW

POET BLOOD 5

The conversation that came and went,
a blind bug sucked into a carnivorous flower.

NO ONE KNOWS

The day mom takes her dress off in the garden and disappears
is the day I wear a dress for the first time and
recognize the smile of a strange country.

That same day
mother secretly picks open the front gate
of a stranger's house that
no one but you lives inside.
On the 100th day I wait for mom
I go underneath the kitchen sink
like melting snow.

Mom pees on top of the snow.
Son, why did you bring me to the rooftop?
Because the wind will blow
all your white hair into the sky.

When snow falls down I paint water on top of my notes.
I could say this water can belong to anybody, but
don't say such a thing. Clearly only a part of my body
flows through your body.

It's been such a long time.
It's so good to have our heads lying side by side on the same pillow.

But Darling, because of the smell of your white hair
I can't get any sleep.
Even if there's not enough sadness to fill you completely,
I go on for a long time.

Like trees, hundreds of thousands of lit candles
that entered your dress caused a mob-like scene.
Like a fragment of a white cloud, you fell asleep inside that crowd.
I'll leave the front gate open when I go out to find you.

Starting from the day you didn't know me,
no one knew
the you that I know.

CAVE STORY

When you try to describe the night by writing it down on the map
water rises little by little
in a village no one has ever been to.

If you spread open a map no one has ever seen
the town that you know disappears.

I

The painter's canvas blooms a sunken world.
The painter's paint restores a flooded town.

The dam is cracked with the painter's finest brush.

But how to restore a town submerged in a work of art?
After pondering the question, the first thing to do
is to paint a town underwater.
Then, drop by drop, you've got to drain the water out.

II

The brush plunges into the water surface.
It whisks deeply as the town sloshes around on the brush.
(On this kind of night you've got to be careful not to let the bone
of yourself get washed away. Never become a resident of the village.
Those people dreamt dreams that lived in the surface of a water used
ages ago.)

Little by little the brush stirs the town into water on the canvas.
However, the town is not seen by other people. Only the painter.
"Again and again it's like pouring water in a painting."
The painter stops and tries to wait
until the water dries in the painting.
"I'll stop painting when the town is revealed!"

III

Water completely fills the painting.
It does not subside.
Many brushes drown.
Each time he faces the painting
the painter has to wait for a sunny day
to hold a funeral for his brush.
He gazes into the water and
recognizes the night that came to visit the bone he calls himself.
People can't understand why he spends so much time

sitting in front of that underwater world.
Rumor has it there's a forest no one has ever stepped into
that sunk inside the water.
A man is painting strange bones dancing in it.

IV

Lots of time flows by.
The painter grows old. Exhausted.
"It would have been better if I hid the town in the water in my eyes."
The painter quietly has a thought.
He will paint an entire night
so no one can enter his painting.
Night slowly flows into the water.
Because the night is painted dark
the man can't find that town again.

Some wanderer departs at night.
He looks for a bone he calls himself.

RIVERS OF TRIVIAL TEARS, ALL FOR THIS

Everyone you get intimate with goes away.
Whenever a spring day dog gets startled
it softly steps on a butterfly with one of its paws.
It barks at the void.

After thinking a bit
about this sense of loss,
after taking a bite of dried sausage,
I finger around some raisin-mix.
I heat pumpkin porridge for 3 minutes.
Just the same. Some time remains.
Is it noon underneath my desk?
Is my pillow still filled with the night?
One time I secretly entered
a stranger's greenhouse
and accidentally saw
the trivial yellow towel
that commemorated a spring harmonica competition.
Somehow a sense of guilt
rose up and made me laugh.
I took a spin around the neighborhood
and that tender sense of guilt disappeared.
The more cheerful my life

the more fearful.
(Is there such a thing as whale-scented toothpaste?)
Therefore I tend a little to my errors.
A ghost is the only thing
I can love concisely.

Rivers of trivial tears, all for this.

Taking these dried boxes
with me every time I move,
carrying stacks of letters a stranger gave me.
I never knew old letters
collect more spouting water than dust.
A letter is someone's silence
drawing a long horizon
toward someone else's silence.
While the place to talk of loss disappears,
all of humanity walks backwards.
If I lower my eyes
the pacing of my backwards walk
is the quiet word's cough.
With this pacing I stuffed the paper
full with my snowy countries, but
both joy and disillusionment
no longer pierce my flesh.
Until these things are indiscernible
I will bloom laziness.

Writing not things that are possible
but what is inevitable.

Erasing not things that are possible
but the inevitable.

That's not it.
No, no. Not that thing but
the steering past of the thing that's not.
Today you are that which flickers sideways.
You going back to your country.
Erasing the country of my departure.
The kiss of a bear.

MIDNIGHT HIGHLIGHTER

A consonant gets lonely easily. If Yellow grows tired with my heart, all to the good. Like how the beak turns blue as soon as the bird dies, you look up your nose underwater and see that tonight is a night when sleep arrives like a sea horse that breathes through its nose under the sea. Erasing a bit of my lips, I try to recall the shapes of the calves of my childhood family. I invent a new word. The bangs of hammers that lay the construction tracks of the longest railway on this earth, vowels. Our world is the world of those who underline the words they walk upon. Like setting free a mosquito after catching it in an empty hand, after painting the mosquito's entire body with a highlighter, oh disharmony! Best regards! Breastbone! Best regards! Come back pitch-black! My poetry rents me the inside of bubbles.

A X L E

It's only right they split up, but
while they give and take nothing
they give and take everything.

Piles of wisdom
find what's wild inside a compass.

Absorbed in the official business
of lips that carry secrets.

Some natures can't be betrayed by coincidence.
Two natures call out
"nature" to each other.

He is H and he is S and
he is S and he is J.

You can't avoid it.
Even if you throw your hands up to hide it.
You, inside the painting
I paint impossibly bright.

0 HOUR RUNWAY

The control tower
can't track the flight path.
All the while,
floating at high altitude, the cockpit
is kept secret from the world.

From now on the plane
must fly outside survey and measurement.
The dashboard is lit with a flame no one has ever seen.
The plane is going to fall to a destination
no one has ever been to.

Like seeing the very first snow

the poet enters that vision—
broadcasting the flight
and the fall.

No picture of homecoming can be revealed.
Night seeps into
cold water rinsing rice and
it becomes a sweet reading room.
Nameless and nonexistent.
In that reading room the poet
erases a rusted foundry.

The person that believes traffic is an organism
arrives at the blank page.
No one speaks of
the forest growing inside the pencil.

With a green skull hung around his neck,
the poet beats
the drum of failure.
The critic
cuts a hole with a knife
in the abdomen of a goldfish.
He chucks the fish back in the tank.

Each to each, experiencing different paths of flight,
the poet and the critic
never meet on the same runway.

100 ACRES OF FARM, 100 ACRES OF FOREST

The scientist touches his stethoscope to the flower pot.
He recalls tombs buried on the seafloor.

A cat carries a lifeless mouse
into a sunflower field.
He scoops the heart out and eats it.

After several years the spider returns.
He presses the stethoscope to his web and

steals a peek through the window of the operating room.
A single flaccid arm.

I dry the dishes indifferently.

iV

-

FEET
ALWAYS
COLD
LiKE
YOU

A LIFE RUMMAGING THROUGH BOOKS

Like a chopstick that accidentally
snuck into a pencil case

it begins.

Like a kid
lightly placing a pencil inside a spoon holder

it ends.

I KNOW

The North Pole train carries echoes, no passengers.
Echoes are all it knows.

A slide made of white marble in an unpopulated town.
Child ghosts hug rabbits on their laps and ride down.

"Did you also ride the North Pole train?
If you make a sad face, you have to wake up from the dream.
We melted. We vanished under our feet.
Only sad bunnies are left. Only sad bunnies grow old.
"Don't leave! The bunnies will get old alone."

"All that'll be left on the slide will be bunny fur."

"Let's pray for snow like old bunnies.
We'll wait for the next North Pole train."

"But who is riding the next North Pole train?"

The North Pole train drops off white blankets. No passengers.
White blankets are all it knows.

"The blankies have arrived.
The bunnies can go inside.
They can fall asleep."

"Between sleeps our sick mom will lay you down.
Open mom's eyes and fly away.
On the North Pole train, fly.
On the North Pole train, fly.
The North Pole train
that you drew on a white blanket while lying down..."

The North Pole train carries echoes, no passengers.
Echoes are all that it knows.

"Between sleeps, bunnies. I know. I know."

I LOVE CONFESSIONS

Water flows out my ears in winter.
I always have this kind of presence
when we break up.

I drink fog.
The passing train is endless.
I read boringly between the lines.

Will my beard grow
while the train goes through this tunnel?

Like a rumor
I visit the various ways of spelling
the tender hair you carry.

You can cry
when your eyes are closed and
you can say "I love you"
when your eyes are open.
What sentence did you write
to capture this sense of presence?

"Buy me a drink!"
Today is Labor Day.

I will stick to your side
like an orange.

When we break up
I'm like the human habit of becoming tender,
but my feet are always cold like you.

I love confessions.

REGISTERING FAMILY TO THE PLACE WHERE FATHER WAS BORN

Can I call a feeling I feel alone
my father's hometown?

Like the times I tried to find my father's hometown,
like a sentence I secretly visited last night,
the borders of my father's hometown disappear
each time I give notice that I moved.

A person that visits their father's hometown
cannot find that sentence again.
In order for this feeling I am feeling right now to quickly pass,
I try to feel the feeling of visiting my father's hometown.
The evidence of my visit will be taken to the cemetery.
It will be written on the tombstone of a nameless swan.

I still haven't seen the sentence with my name on it.
Your sentence doesn't know your family registry.
(All of your open eyes inhabit that empty space.)
If I've never been to your father's hometown
do I have to say I haven't met you?
If I secretly visited your father's hometown
do I have to say you're my echo?

Father fell down at the bathhouse.
He can't remember the family.registry.
At the neighborhood office
is a pissed off son
asking his father to state his hometown correctly.
Even though he has never seen his father
who continues to call out weird places as if they are his hometown,
a baby has been born.
The son has to register his baby's place
even if that baby
is someone he hasn't yet seen.

DUCK DOWN, BUT NOT
FROM THE UGLY DUCKLING

Duck down flies. A duck down parka.
One time in the middle of the night
I took a duvet out the house
and discarded it in the forest.

White duck feathers on the stump of a tree.
The piece of a bookstand I swallowed
after taking a beating
turned into hiccups.

A child grabs an old man by his pocket.
The old man is trying to shut the flood gates to the reservoir.
The child asks, "Old man, when people die,
does blood flow out their mouths?"

"If you lose the game where you put
a rock on your foot and run until you pass the line
the penalty is that wherever we go
you get to drag me by the wrist."

Someone who came to our house for the first time said,
"Wow, your house is such a big rock!"

There are a ton of ants at our house.
All of them have black, thin waists.

The duck down parka
that I found on the trunk of a tree
sunk with the person who jumped to the bottom of the dam.
I followed duck feathers that fell in the forest.
I picked up the jacket and wore it secretly until high school.
To repay the owner of the jacket
I jumped into the reservoir.

Like duck down poking out
spiteful blood floats to you.

A man floats to the surface of the water
like hiccups.

WHEN I GO TO TOUCH
YOUR SKIN

When I go to touch your skin
like I am hiding the most hot
genitals

the bird that lives
borrowing my skin
will never have descendants.

The poet has sex in that flock of birds.

Can the bird that rises up in this sentence
become an accident?
No, it won't.

More than a document,
baby dinosaurs
pecking and eating poetry
fill up an accident.

They are like some sentence
a bird left behind.

SHIP BUILDER

Seagulls stuffed underneath my desk.
When I imagine rocks I get happy.
I like carpet when it's burned black.
Collected in a box,
the soft, front paws of cats.
A storm is only a storm
when it smashes every window
like sesame seeds.
A tsunami wheezes inside this pencil.
I head into
a broken-down engine room
and hula hoop.
Like plankton I fill with breath.
Bedrooms spread out.
They sink.

1 SHEEP, 2 SHEEP

My name is Shepherd Boy. I have to go find my flock of sheep before it gets dark.

I blow on my pipe and collect my flocks of sleepy sheep. They gather on the tip of my pipe. I put on fake eyelids and call the eyes of the wolf hiding in my flocks of sheep "snowstorm." Tonight I have to take a snowstorm to the country of dazzling ice.

My name is Shepherd Boy. I have a long blue beard. The horse's hoofs that belong to poor me thicken like the shape of your toes. My horse's hoofs go on holiday. They become tens of thousands of clouds. They become tens of thousands of towns. They are black magic wizards. They are daughters that no one knows. At night the horse's hoofs that belong to poor me are the character of the saddest country that I know. They lie down.

My name is Shepherd Boy. I've got to pull everything out of my pockets before nightfall. In order for my flock of sheep not to lose the path, they grab and hold my pockets. There are many boys that beat drums in my notebook. Those boys tell lies every day. They cry every day. The boys who can't stop crying turn their pockets inside out. They wait for flocks of sheep.

My name is Shepherd Boy. My sheep have dry throats because my lies are poor. The lies of poor me bring you into the forest to feed. They bring you the soft water and feed you the green grass and fresh fruit. They place the butterflies that rose out of the surface of water into your ears. Sitting on a boulder, I pull hard bread out my pocket. This is my drum. I release my flocks of sheep. I say this is the poor atmosphere of poor me and—

Mom, I still haven't been able to name my beautiful flocks of sheep. *Son, they are the words that hide in soft, white fur.* Mom, it's because the inside of words are cold. *Son, the flocks of sheep that you lost, you will begin to see them living in hiding inside some crack in a rock. The water in your breath that starts to freeze is the sheep.* Mom, why did you lose me in the valley of winds? *Your pockets became big like the wind.* Mom, I remember you even when I'm dying. Mom, I don't want my pocket to freeze. When I die I want to become a big drum. *Son, those words are like sheep fur. They ascend a winding staircase into your body.*

My name is Shepherd Boy. My horse hoofs that can't sleep are breathless. Look at the sky and you'll find my flocks. My flocks of sheep file toward the beach. Snow falls on their heads. The subjects of some kingdom console the words carved into a stone by building a fire on it. Flocks of sheep fall to earth. They lift their hooves and rub their sleepy eyes. One sheep . . . two sheep . . . my atmosphere.

BEACH SCHOOL BUS

I have two pale feet
when I go to the beach.
When I walk to the sky
my feet turn white.

LIKE WATER LEAKING

—Paju

Sometimes darkness arrives
like leaking water.

Water leaks into this room
as if it is the afterlife.

The life that I know
completely fills
the sound of leaking water.
I quietly crouch.
A year warps the door knob
while water leaks.

As if the afterlife fills in my sentences,
my melancholic ankles sleep
clenching the door handle
because they are lonely.

Outside the door
a stag beetle
sets
its rib to a bone.

BLUE BLOOD

—for my wife

The first time your breast went into my hand
you hugged my waist like a wild goose
and tried to fly away.

If you've got to to eat boiled baby legs during an insurrection,
you've got to do what you've got to do, but
if a man's blood has to be tougher than a mountain,
you say you want to live
following my flesh and touching my ribs.

I forget things all the time. Even the road back home.
We should both admit that I forgot about your grave.
Whatever. We are foam bubbles born in our mothers' water.

You say that in order to write poetry you have to spit out the dust of stones.
Only write poetry that goes in and out of your bones.
You say you can't make lightning or change the color of leaves with a
    rice cooker.
You say drop that crying kid in the woods.
You say don't tremble in front of a spicy hot soup!

I am someone that suffers from poetry
and my poetry is the color of mulberry.
It makes the body itchy.
I am sorrowful each time my foot brushes your foot inside the blanket.
I am like the mugwort bird that failed at singing songs.
But graves and spring rain are two things
I can't let go.

NOTES:

The Reason I Turn My Back and Walk Away is based on a title of a poem by Baek Seok.

Kim Kyung Ju is a Seoul-based poet, dramatist, and performance artist. His poetry and essays are widely anthologized in South Korea, and his plays have been produced in several countries. He has written and translated over a dozen books of poetry, essays, and plays and has been the recipient of many prizes and awards, including the Korean government's Today's Young Artist Prize and the Kim Su-yong Contemporary Poetry Award.

Jake Levine is an American translator, poet, and scholar. He received both his BA and MFA from the University of Arizona and is currently Abd in a PhD program in comparative literature at Seoul National University. He works as an assistant professor of creative writing at Keimyung University and as a lecturer at the Literature Translation Institute of Korea. He is the assistant editor at Acta Koreana and the editor for the Korean poetry series Moon Country published by Black Ocean.

ABOUT THE SERIES

Black Ocean :: Moon Country publishes new English translations of contemporary Korean poetry by both mid-career and up-and-coming poets who debuted after the IMF crisis. By introducing work that comes out of our shared milieu, this series not only aims to widen the field of contemporary Korean poetry available in English translation, but also to challenge orientalist, neo-colonial, and national literature discourses. Our hope is that readers will inhabit these books as bodies of experience rather than view them as objects of knowledge, that they will allow themselves to be altered by them, and emerge from the page with eyes that seem to see "a world that belongs to another star."*

*From the poem "Moon Country Mischief" by Kim Soo-young